in the shelter
of the covered bridge

Jan 29, 2016 'green apples - Malone'   Jane Tims

in the shelter of the covered bridge

poems and drawings by
Jane Spavold Tims

Chapel Street Editions
Woodstock, New Brunswick

Copyright © 2017 Jane Spavold Tims
All rights reserved

This is a work of fiction. Names, characters, places and incidents are products of the author's imagination or used fictitiously and are not to be construed as real. Any resemblance to actual events, locales, organisations or persons, living or dead, is entirely coincidental.

Published by
Chapel Street Editions
150 Chapel Street
Woodstock, NB E7M 1H4

www.chapelstreeteditions.com

Library and Archives Canada Cataloguing in Publication

Tims, Jane Spavold, author, illustrator
    In the shelter of the covered bridge / poems and drawings by
Jane Spavold Tims.

Includes index.
ISBN 978-1-988299-10-5 (softcover)

    I. Title.

PS8639.I568I5 2017   C811'.6   C2017-905804-5

Cover illustration: "apple tree, Malone Bridge" by Jane Spavold Tims

The text is set in Iowan Old Style, a typeface designed by John Downer and released by Bitstream in 1990. It is modeled after earlier revivals of Jenson and Griffo.

Book design by Brendan Helmuth

dedication

to Michael
who planted some of those trees
beside the Millstream River

"… Take binoculars and a bird book (birds love the covered bridge sites). You will never hear more caroling, chirping, fluting and twittering …"

Lyn Harrington and Richard Harrington
Covered Bridges of Central and Eastern Canada

Contents

Foreword i
Preface iii
Acknowledgements v
liminal spaces 1
    tangle 3
    under the bridge 5
    sun shadow, rain shadow, wind shadow 6
    trinket box 7
    punctuation 8
    map 10
    dripline 11
    location, location 13
    interloper 15
    green 16
    web 17
notch of a lily pad 19
    summer song 20
    Bear Creek Meadow by canoe 23
    signs 25
    beaver slap 27
    at the entrance to the covered bridge 29
    dragonflies 31
    scribble 32
    hawk and pigeon 33
    tree swallow 35
    geography 36

    free-range 37
    not a humming bird 39
    on the north-east wall 40
    shelter 41
    sticky tongue, tail prop, zygodactyl feet 42

grit of a blade 43
    bunches of bitter 45
    kissing bridge 47
    'PHOEBE' 49
    'LANA + ...' 50
    forever 51
    confluence 53
    'LEIK 1931' 54
    black horse 55
    crossing 1942 56
    holes 58
    throb 60

a blade of grass between thumbs 63
    conjunction – February 21, 2015 65
    ptarmigan hunter 67
    'TOM MOUSE' #1 69
    'TOM MOUSE' #2 70
    wind enters 73
    time-stamped 75
    a spider waits 77
    samara storm 78
    'I AM THE WIND' 79
    mystery 81

gaps between boards 83
    ceiling of stars 84
    push 85

    carving 87
    surveillance 89
    break-in #1. 91
    break-in #2. 93
    'chikin'. 94
    'AJS 1932' 96
    wobble. 98
    dry wood. 99
    Aaron Clark Bridge on the Canaan River 101
    cars discouraged. 103

a loose board rattles 105
    dry wind. 107
    sound of the mill 108
    posters 109
    keeping watch 111
    pastoral 112
    family drive, when we were five 113
    disarranged 115
    delay 116
    respiration 117
    dark mirror 119
    maintenance 120
    renewal 121
    morning 122
    thalweg 123

Afterword 125
Notes on the Drawings. 127
Sources 130
Sources for Epigraphs 131
About the Author. 132
Index 133

Foreword

A few years ago I was racing around New Brunswick like a rally driver in search of the finish line. I had a deadline to meet. I was to find and photograph every covered bridge in the province. At the time, 2010, there were still sixty-three in place. In the 40s, there were over three hundred. It was a crazy time, but a fun one. So with my GPS charged, the Department of Transportation's website directions printed out, and the New Brunswick Atlas in hand, I was off and running.

When I saw the manuscript for Jane's book, suddenly memories of things I had only glimpsed, or held for the moment, came flooding back. I had enjoyed the challenge of finding the bridges. Once I had to ford a stream, waist-deep in icy water. Another time I ended up sliding down a steep riverbank like an otter to get the angle I needed – forgetting that the climb back up was going to be much harder. Sometimes I felt like a birder trying to tick off every bird on a very long life-list. But there also were moments when I was stopped in my tracks: the setting was just too beautiful, or the sound of a waterfall just too catching. And then I was again on the move in search of the next bridge.

Now, with Jane's poems and sketches in hand, I am allowed to stop and linger at each bridge, to feel its presence in the landscape, its place in the history of the local community. At each bridge Jane visits, her poems capture a moment that often goes unnoticed by human eyes – small things like spider webs, animal tracks and dragonflies. But she also notes our passage as well: names carved into wood pledging undying love, memories of horse drawn carriages clattering across wooden floors.

in the shelter of the covered bridge, gives us a chance to stop, to listen and to feel a bit of the magic that comes from slowing down and spending time with something – the magic that comes from looking and feeling and being present.

Brian Atkinson

Brian Atkinson is a professional photographer. He has published five books, including *New Brunswick's Covered Bridges, Miramichi: River of Character,* and *Sustaining the Gaze: When Images Tremble.* Over the past twenty-five years he has travelled widely in Canada and to some seventy countries, often on assignment for international agencies or Canadian media.

Preface

Where I live in rural New Brunswick, driving through a covered bridge is a daily occurrence. The sounds of the tires on the decking, the glimpses of river and sunlight between boards, the fun of seeing a family fishing and the sight of a groundhog carrying her kit across entryway of the bridge – these are touch-stones for my existence.

The inspiration for this book came in 2015, when my husband and I crossed the local covered bridge, the Patrick Owens Bridge across the Rusagonis Stream, and startled a rabbit. The rabbit raced through the bridge in front of the truck. I can still see the shadow of his long ears and the scurry of his feet. Since the incident occurred during the February 21, 2015 conjunction of Venus and Mars, with the sickle moon just above the planets, I thought of all the legends about the hare and the moon. This led to the poem "conjunction" and a question about what other plants and animals find shelter in or around our covered bridges in New Brunswick.

My husband and I carried out the field work for the book during 2015. We focused on covered bridges in the entire St. John River Valley, but we also visited bridges in Charlotte and Westmorland Counties. Travelling around the province, visiting covered bridges and paying special attention to the nearby wild life, was an ideal way to spend a spring and summer in New Brunswick. Some bridges were easy to find, others a challenge. Each bridge contributed its own personality, history and component flora and fauna.

The covered bridge is endangered in New Brunswick. In 1900, there were about 400 covered bridges in the province. By 1944, there were only 320. In 1992, when Glen, Michael and I visited some of the bridges for Canada's 125th birthday, there were 71. In 2017, as I write this, there are only 59 remaining. Vandalism, flood, accident, fire and age claim more bridges every few years.

One of the reasons for preserving covered bridges is the diversity of habitat they create for plants, animals and other living things. Within the bridge are surfaces for spiders to build webs and crannies for mosses to grow. Fish swim in the cooler waters or deep pools beneath the bridge. Mice find refuge in cubbyholes within bridge architecture and swallows find surfaces to build their nests. At one time, horses were regular visitors to covered bridges. Humans also spend time within the covered bridge – couples meet in the privacy of the bridge, kids go there to "hang out" and communities celebrate, holding weddings and community suppers inside the covered bridge.

Acknowledgements

My first thanks goes to my companion in my travels, my husband Glen. He was the pilot; I was the navigator. My directions – "Stop. Turn here. No there. This can't be right. Take this road." – were often a challenge. Glen also checked each bridge for bird nests and each shoreline for tracks. And he listened to every poem and offered suggestions.

Our travels in 2015 reminded us both of an earlier project: back in 1992, we travelled with our son Michael to many of New Brunswick's covered bridges as a project under CANADA 125, to celebrate Canada's 125th anniversary. Our notes and the pencil rubbings from those visits provided some of the reference material for my poems.

A big smile goes to my brother Lee who shared his memories of crossing the Hartland Covered Bridge with my nieces and nephew when they were children and wrote his own poem to assist the story! Thanks also to my sister Heather and her husband Denis who travelled with us to some of the covered bridges in Kings County. Denis also took my author photo and has helped me with photography over the years.

Working with my publisher, Chapel Street Editions, on this and my first book of poetry *within easy reach* (2016) was so enjoyable. I appreciate the gentle guidance of Keith Helmuth and his love of all things associated with the St. John River. Thank you to Ellen Helmuth for her warmth, her reading of my work and her attention to the background detail. And thanks especially to Brendan Helmuth, the book's designer, for his encouragement, endless patience and artist's eye.

I am grateful to Shari Andrews for her advice and comments on many of the poems in the manuscript. My participation with her in the mentoring program is thanks to the Writers' Federation of New Brunswick.

I also thank the members of my writing groups, Fictional Friends and Wolf Tree Writers, for listening to the poems and commenting. I particularly want to thank Dr. Kathleen McConnell, Department of English, St. Thomas University for helping me with the sonnet form. Also, thanks to Dr. Roger Moore, Professor Emeritus, St. Thomas University, and members of the Moncton Blue Pencil Group for comments on some of the poems.

Throughout the project, I used the New Brunswick Department of Transportation and Infrastructure's very helpful website about New Brunswick's covered bridges. The list provides directions for finding the bridges as well as information on the architecture and age of each bridge by County. http://www2.gnb.ca/content/gnb/en/departments/dti/bridges_ferries/content/covered_bridges.html

The wild life in the vicinity of the Benton Bridge was particularly interesting and challenging. Dr. Don McAlpine, New Brunswick Museum, helped me identify the clearwing hawk moth. Dr. Stephen Clayden, also with the Museum, identified the lichens growing on the side of the bridge and shared information about other lichens in the project. Nelda Craig helped verify the identity of the stonefly nymphs on the exterior walls of the bridge. She also made some comments on the New Brunswick rivers and streams she knows so well.

Facebook is a place to meet others with similar interests and so I was inspired by the public group "Covered Bridges New Brunswick" moderated by Clarence Ball. The forum gave me a place to post bridge photos and a chance for feedback. I would also like to thank the followers of my Blog site www.nichepoetryandprose.wordpress.com for their interest and many comments.

Some of the poems have been published in *The Cormorant* ("I am the Wind", "summer song"), *Canadian Stories* ("Bear Creek Meadow by Canoe", "interloper", "geography" published as "from the window of the covered bridge"), *Existere* ("TOM MOUSE #1" published as "TOM MOUSE", "TOM MOUSE #2") and *Galleon* ("dry wood", "'AJS 1932'"). Other poems have appeared at www.nichepoetryandprose.wordpress.com. The poem "sun shadow, rain shadow, wind shadow" was inspired by Brian Atkinson's photo of the Back Creek #2 (Hoyt Station) Covered Bridge.

Some of the poems appeared in the manuscript "mnemonic", winner of the Alfred G. Bailey Prize in the 2016 Writers' Federation of New Brunswick Writing Competition.

I am grateful to artsnb (The New Brunswick Arts Board) for the support of a Creations Grant during the writing and preparation of the manuscript.

liminal spaces

> "… The carriageway under our feet was dark except for the patch of moon …"
>
> Brian Doyle
Covered Bridge

'tangle - Darlings Island Covered Bridge'   Jane Tims

tangle

> Darlings Island Bridge

thoughts muddle
under tremble of light
lifted from the river

ideas caught in the frail
net of a fishing line
tossed to the rafters

or a spider's web
at the peak, segmented
as a string of lights

and shadows, unmatched
freshwater pearls, the liquid
notes of a thrush, and trills perplex

snarled as a leader and bobber
miscast, tangled in overhead
wires above the braid of the river

plaited as the scent of two roses, double pink
and single pale, skitter of maple keys
caught between rattle of loose

boards and braces, inhale
a swallow enters and leaves
flight path as simple as follow [1]

---

[1] The Darlings Island Bridge crosses a tributary of the Hammond River near Nauwigewauk, Kings County, in the lowland area where the Hammond River meets with the Kennebecasis. Built in 1914, the bridge is not in service but used as a park. From the covered bridge you can almost touch the stone parapet of the new concrete bridge. When I think of this bridge, I remember wind and birdsong, the whisper of maple keys, and a white chicken foraging at the entry to the bridge!

under the bridge

> French Village Bridge
> Hammond River #2

river keeps its width and depth
does not cringe as it slides
beneath the bridge

maple seedlings sprout
in a thin row
at the base of the abutment

grasses on the far shore
crowd in soil built
from rotting maple keys

plants dip in stature
where light shadow
meets rain shadow [2]

---

[2] Built in 1912, the French Village Bridge, near Quispamsis, Kings County, once crossed the Hammond River. Near the former location of the bridge, deposits of sand on a broad shoreline make this a popular bathing spot. When we visited, the entryway to the bridge was crowded with wildflowers – wild roses, vetch, yellow rattle and bladder campion.

In 2016, the French Village Bridge (Hammond River #2) was severely damaged when a loaded excavator broke through the bridge. As a result, the bridge was removed.

sun shadow, rain shadow, wind shadow

>   Hoyt Station Bridge
>   Back Creek #2

beneath   the Back Creek Bridge   where
direct light and raindrops never reach
sun shadow   rain shadow   wind shadow
make a lull in the   shoreline vegetation – no fern
or meadowsweet, or mullein, or goldenrod

the tops of grasses draw a curve
against the abutment
shorter, shorter
shortest
longer, longest
necessary adjustment
to partitioning of light
more generous at the southern edge

perpetual shade and the soil is starved
for moisture, a soaking at highest water
a gap where stones expose their angles
and the shore assembles a bar of sand
driftwood gathers, a pointed beaver stick
ruin of a fence from a dairy farm upriver [3]

---

[3]   The Hoyt Station Bridge, near Hoyt Station in Sunbury County, was built in 1936. The bridge crosses Back Creek, where it meanders across a broad floodplain on its way to the South Branch of the Oromocto River.

trinket box

> Pont Boniface
> Green River #3

the wooden bridge
is a trinket box
moss-lined and crammed
with purple petals,
vetch and fireweed
leaflets of meadow rue and fern

dogwood berries are scattered
pearls, dolls' eyes watching
a waxwing select
bluebottles and mayflies
above the river

swallows on telephone lines
threaded by wire [4]

---

[4] The Boniface Bridge was built in 1925 over the Green River near Saint-Basile, Madawaska County. The name of the river is from the French *Rivière Verte* for the colour of the water. While we were at the bridge, we watched the birds swoop back and forth over the river, catching insects.

punctuation

> Bell Bridge
> South Oromocto River #3

cars scoot through the bridge
double honk, leave black marks
hyphenation on floorboards

the hiker shakes his head
leans in to examine initials, engraved
made elegant by punctuation

studies firedots on the abutment
Caloplaca lichen hugs its substrate
loves its bits of calcium

red spots are drops of ink –
stop and watch the river
comma swirls on water

exclamation marks on boards
excavated by woodpeckers
parentheses around nests of swallows

dots and dashes
where old boards criss-cross
let sunlight through [5]

---

[5] Bell Bridge at Juvenile Settlement near Hoyt, Sunbury County, crosses the South Oromocto River over steep banks and plunging water. The bridge, built in 1931, is in an isolated location, surrounded by coniferous woods. The name Oromocto is from the Wolastoqiyik *Well-a-mook'-took* meaning 'good or deep river (for canoeing navigation).'

The lichen *Caloplaca* sp. is also known as firedot because of the spotted red of the spore bodies. These lichens love calcium carbonate and often grow on concrete.

As we explored the bridge a car crossed and honked once, a tradition for some folks when they drive across a covered bridge in New Brunswick.

map

Before I leave, I rest
on the retaining wall.
Study rocks overgrown

by continents and islands
of yellow map lichen –
Rhizocarpon geographicum.

The map is worn and faded
folded and torn
by snow ploughs,

ice scour and frost.
With one fingernail I worry
a patch of lichen, edged by spores.

Land bordered by shoreline,
featureless – without mountains,
streams, meadows or roads.

Tires tremble on boards.
Tectonic plates. Wind rattles
from north to south.

I too am saxicolous, crustose.
I cross the bridge
and drive. [6]

---

[6] *Rhizocarpon geographicum* (L.) DC., also known as the 'map lichen,' grows in patches on exposed stone. The lichen is crustose, in the form of a dry hard layer adhering closely to the substrate. The body of the lichen is bordered by a rim of black spores. Adjacent patches give the impression of a map. Saxicolous means 'living among the rocks.'

dripline

Rain slips from the roof of the bridge
slides from the edge of corrugated steel.
Partitions river into upstream
and down, opaque
and transparent, dead calm
and riffle, dark and light.

Through the curtain of gathered rain
I hear her voice, *'Remember.'* But all I know
are three trout and gravels, perpendicular
rocks, embedded in amber water.
Veil of water disconnects – a year ago last winter
and tomorrow afternoon.

Wall of water crosses river
linear, liminal, shore to shore. [7]

---

[7] Liminal means occupying a position at, or on both sides of, a boundary or threshold.

March 14, 2012   'Coltsfoot'   Jane Tims

location, location

coltsfoot leaves, beaten back from the carriageway
by cars coming and going, new soil settles
from the dregs of water seeping rock to rock

seedlings sprout in fines from the road –
tire dust, road salt and sand
barbules of pigeon feathers, guano

new apartment, new neighborhood, mindful
of commute, school location, walking paths
nearest green space, proximity to crime

reach for light, shrink from the shadow
of the north face, avoid the madness
of spring flood where roots can drown

we climb, vine by stem
gain hold in gaps
and crannies in the cribwork

grasped by the hands of barefoot
children reach, step over rocks
afternoon swim in the river [8]

---

8 The 'fines' are the smallest particles of soil, technically those that pass through a #200 sieve.

April 18, 2016 'watching the bridge'   Jane Tims

interloper

> Baker Brook #2

movement quivers silence, wind lull
in the hush of rain, my hand
disturbs the drip line, quiets the trickle
a drop and the river departs

in waves, a white-throat sings
seven notes and is still
a robin, long grass in her beak
hesitates to enter the bridge, add to her nest

timid, a deer in the hayfield
ponders the tunnel
shadows she has not seen before
framed where I sit on the railing, try

to be motionless, not to shiver
not to turn boredom
into walking, make small
adjustments for comfort

a crow perches
on one round bale of hay
lengthens its neck
croaks a warning [9]

---

9 Baker Brook #2 Bridge was built in 1939 at Morneault Settlement in Madawaska County and is no longer in service. It stands next to the modern concrete bridge, in a wide valley, surrounded by hay fields and rolling forested hills. Baker Brook flows into the St. John River.

green

> Smithtown Bridge
> Hammond River #3

Plastic pail, pink
with green flowers
half-buried in sand.

Colour echo of rocks
red and green
in ankle-deep water.

Algae builds in shallows.
Swimmers feet test each rock for slime.
And up in the bridge

a green-bottle fly crawls
in and out between wall boards
not touching. [10]

---

[10] The Smithtown Bridge was built near Damascus, Kings County in 1914. Where it crosses the Hammond River there is a small sandy beach, popular with local families. When we visited the water was shallow and a bloom of algae was building in the eddies along the shoreline.

web

after spinning
after rain
I am purveyor of worlds

peer through my web
through eight hundred drops
at inverted images

each a replica
of roof, wall and passageway
end post and beam

chains of lenses
ocular spokes
and strands

built a web to catch
the rain? I don't think so
but insects never came to call

so I am content
with captured
covered bridges, over-turned

swimmers, girls gone fishing
and the occasional
Chevrolet

notch of a lily pad

"... And the lilies revived, and the dragon-fly
Came back to dream on the river ..."

Elizabeth Barrett Browning
"A Musical Instrument"

summer song

    Patrick Owens Bridge
    Rusagonis River #2

Sunbury County
sings in its sleep
      purple vetch
      hop clover
    bluegrass
at the roadside

hay in rows
      a staff empty of song
        round bails
    and their shadows
half notes for an oboe

honey bee
ditty in the pink
      old fashioned roses
       bid country roads
    enter the covered bridge
glimpses between planking
rock music on the water
tires drumming loose boards

deer look up

cattle low in the meadow

      owl to whitethroat

        counterpoint

      lupins pepper the air

    rushes by the Rusagonis

north and south

big moon crescendo

      over Sunpoke

   firefly

follies in the fern [11]

---

11   Located in Rusagonis, Sunbury County, the Patrick Owens Bridge over the Rusagonis Stream was built in 1909. A full-length side window allows a view of the river upstream where the North and South Branches of the river meet. The Wolastoqiyik name for the Rusagonis Stream was *Tes-e-gwan'-ik* meaning 'meeting with the main stem.'

Bear Creek Meadow by canoe

    Patrick Owens Bridge
    Rusagonis River #2

downstream of the bridge
we make a brief portage
to the other side of the beaver dam
over poles and patted mud
up to the quiet pond

        bow
        bleached by white water
        parts green

        paddles
        pitted by rocks and snags
        spoon soup

frog's eyes
solemn in the harbour-notch of lily pads
audit our passing

our voices
heed the diminishing echo
honour the whisper of wild rice
        the edgewise touching
          of nymphaea and nuphar

we are pliant as stems of pickerel weed
gentle on the water
    threaded by dragonflies
    slim blue needles
    drawn by striding insects
    over a cloak of water shield

the oval pads are a puzzle
part, return to their places

    no trace of our passing

signs

on the shore in gravel
lacuna-deep growls of river
bears and foxes
crows and raccoons
leave their sign

bowels emptied and tracks
scat solidified with bone
berries, fur and feathers
tapered, with a flourish
or segmented as rope

lift the river grass to find
impressions in mud
repeated combinations
of pads and tarsals, phalanges
fingers and claws

other spoor beneath the bridge
under corbels, beside stonework
covert spaces for kill
and feed and wallow
feasts, hid from jealous eyes

Aug. 20, 2012   'Yellow Pond-lily'   Jane Tims

beaver slap

    Bloomfield Creek Bridge

bank beaver swims
under the covered bridge
up and down the creek
course designed to confuse

entry to his dwelling, humble rubble
haphazard sticks, heaped against the shore
hidden by stalks of pickerel weed, yarrow on the shore
spatterdock tucked into the slash of lily pads

cobwebs tremble, a swallow veers
cars thud and rumble and honk
ring of a hammer, nail-studded sun
at ten the church bell clangs

body scissor
tail lift
slap! [12]

---

[12] Bloomfield Creek Bridge, near Bloomfield, Kings County, was built in 1917. Bloomfield Creek is a tributary of the Kennebecasis River. Where the bridge crosses, the creek is winding and marshy, and bank beavers build their lodges against the shorelines. Carvings inside the bridge include an elongated sun enclosing a line of five rusty nails.

Dec. 29, 2011 'three studies of a groundhog Cambridge Narrows, July, 2011' © Jane Tims

at the entrance to the covered bridge

Patrick Owens Bridge
Rusagonis River #2

1.

a groundhog totes her kit
by the scruff of the neck
compliant gather of fur

pushes through rose bushes
crosses asphalt, finds an opening
between guard rails

the bridge a barrier
to natural, more secretive
passage

she risks the car in the bridge
the truck waiting to cross
the hawk in the elm, sharpening his beak

2.

in the thicket of burdock
under guard rails, between posts
a thick and hairy question mark quivers
where the grey squirrel hides
convinced he is safe
from the rush
of the morning
commute

3.

dark choke-cherries, scarlet keys of ash
hang, counterweight to summer
blue jays strip the branches, berry by berry
v-beaks and hollow throats

dragonflies

1.

near the covered bridge
the insect population dwindles
dragonfly-thin

2.

the red dragonfly, thorax
bronze, wings transparent
settles on the bridge
beaded eyes will never see
darning needle abdomen

3.

blue dragonfly floats
on air, slender sapphire stick –
pin iridescence

scribble

> Salmon Bridge
> Kennebecasis River #7.5

The robin, chary. Her beak drips
with wet meadow grass and chickweed.
She clucks, longs to add another strand
to her nest in the rafters,

woven with the trill of a scribble bird,
a winter wren delirious. And downy
woodpeckers, wing-flare and scrabble,
flirt in the willows, weeping.

A warbler (yellow blur-bird)
and a red-wing, *toweeeee*.
Pink roses, meadowsweet
chip, chip, chip, so-wary-we

and beneath the bridge
in soft mud beside pulled grass
the bleary track of a black bear
claws and pads [13]

---

13   When not in service, a covered bridge is designated with a '.5' number – the Salmon Bridge was once Kennebecases River #8. The bridge, near Sussex, Kings County, was built across the Kennebecasis River in 1908. Today it is used as a rest area. In the absence of traffic, wild life has occupied the bridge. Virginia creeper covers one corner of the roof and rose bushes crowd the edges of the road. In mid-May, when we were there, birds were busy in and around the bridge, preferring to be left to their own springtime activities.

hawk and pigeon

    Salmon Bridge
    Kennebecasis River #7.5

> "… inside the Salmon River Bridge near Sussex last Sunday … a small hawk … feeding on a dead pigeon …" [14]

hawk sets talons and plucks
one clump of feathers
quick survey and another
adjustment of claws

    a struggle and still
    one eye blinks

bloody beak stretches integument
tears membrane, tugs at tendon

feathers
and
after
feathers
fluff
and tumble
scatter
along
the length
of the bridge

---

14 'Hawk Enjoys Meal Inside Bridge', New Brunswick Covered Bridges, http://64.118.87.14/~nblight/bridges/index.html, February 18, 2004.

March 6, 2016   'tree swallow'   Jane Tims

tree swallow

> Hoyt Station Bridge
> Back Creek #2

twitter, liquid as water
simmers above the floodplain
seeps and shallows

three circle glide
three quick flaps
to climb and glide again

blue-green-black
with a white throat
quick tuck into the bridge

a *twee* and a flutter
a perch in rafters
rest and a short run

to ram the inside boards
neither frightened
nor confused

the goal? the blue-bottle
on the inside-shadow-side
of sun-warm boards

geography

> McCann Bridge
> Digdeguash River #4

bedrock tilted
nudges the river sideways
dictates the way of the road

sun shines on amber water
and fingerlings glide over gravels
slim shadows
mimic the passage
of their fishes
show us the way
to navigate shivers
between rocks

water striders
in sets of six dots
skip across the shallows [15]

---

15 The McCann Bridge at Rollingdam, Charlotte County was built in 1938 across the Digdeguash River. The water is coloured by water-soluble tannins originating in wetlands in the upper reaches of the watershed.

free-range

Darlings Island Bridge

a white rooster
red wattles and crown
pecks at the weed-edge

random path
from sunny yard
to shaded bridge

not in service
no need to shrink against the wall
to keep an eye out

the best pickings
in grooves
between floor boards

not a humming bird

Benton Bridge
Eel River #3

wing blur in the lilac
threshold of the bridge
scent-thick and purple
nothing as it seems

not a bee or bird – a hawk moth
hummingbird clearwing
Hemaris thysbe
wings a blood-stained veil

lilac thryse to lilac thryse
side-slip, hover
nectar thirst
fierce harvest [16]

---

16 The Benton Bridge, built in 1927, crosses the Eel River at Benton, York County. The bridge is in an open area of houses, hay fields and a mowed picnic park. Insect life dominated our visit. A huge lilac on one end of the bridge was busy with hawk moths and eastern tiger swallowtail butterflies. Stonefly nymphs covered the boards on the outside of the bridge – the nymphs are a life stage of a primitive group of insects whose presence indicates good or excellent water quality.

The clearwing hawk moth is a type of sphinx moth often mistaken for a hummingbird or bumblebee. The moth hovers as it feeds on flower nectar. The name *thysbe* is from Ovid's tragic story of the lovers Thisbe and Pyramus. The body of the moth has transparent reddish wings reminiscent of Thisbe's blood-soaked veil. In the story Pyramus finds the veil and incorrectly assumes Thisbe is dead.

The flower cluster of the lilac is of the type known as a thryse. The thryse grows in a particular pattern, resulting in an elongated flower stem with lateral clusters of flowers.

on the north-east wall

    Benton Bridge
    Eel River #3

on the shaded side of the covered bridge
the walls are clothed, furred
in lichen

boreal oakmoss
      yellow-grey and goose-fleshed
     (*Evernia mesomorpha*)
and burred horsehair
      bristled, toasted and tangled
     (*Bryoria furcellata*)

thrive on the weathered boards
from eaves to river they follow
the runnelways of damp
cool on the dark side of the bridge
bark and branches their usual home [17]

---

17   Boreal oakmoss (*Evernia mesomorpha*) and burred horsehair (*Bryoria furcellata*) are common lichens, usually found on trees in open coniferous woods or on scraggy trees in bogs.

shelter

the engine dies – after midnight
not far from home

snow builds on track
eyelash and mitten

wind conceals the road
sweeps the bridge

enter, a lull and chill subsides
bright of snow subdued

no solitude – a mouse ticked
off, her hibernation interrupted

and ghosts carve names, spray
broad epithets in purple

inspire defiance, kick me
out, into the storm

sticky tongue, tail prop, zygodactyl feet

Smyth Bridge
South Oromocto River #2

morning chorus, chain of birdsong
(white-throat mnemonic and robin melodic
wheezy phoebe, junco click)
grubs mumble, coil in rotting wood

beneath drum roll, jagged percussion
black jackhammer, hairy woodpecker excavates
bridge soffit, sugar maple stump
sticky tongue, tail prop, zygodactyl feet

beak throws wood chips, heaps sawdust and splinters
black and white a grey smudge
bright head-bars a red blur, tap a stammer
steady stutter, busyspeak [18]

---

18 Built in 1912, the Smyth Bridge, also known as the Mill Settlement Bridge, crosses the South Branch of the Oromocto River at Mill Settlement, near Hoyt, Sunbury County. In summer the waters beneath the bridge are shallow and white with rapids. The bridge is isolated, in woods of fir, spruce, white birch and red maple. There is a small parking area on the north bank where local people picnic. The excavations of a woodpecker have created lines of oval cavities between the boards covering the gable ends of the bridge. Woodpecker feet are zygodactyl, arranged for clinging, with first and forth toes facing backwards and second and third toes facing forwards.

The mnemonic is a memory device used to help in remembering. The mnemonic 'I love dear Canada, Canada, Canada' helps birdwatchers remember the song of the white-throated sparrow.

grit of a blade

"... We'll build
  Our bridge across it, and the bridge shall be
  Our arm thrown over it asleep beside it ..."

Robert Frost
"West-Running Brook"

Jan. 29, 2016 'choke-cherries at Becaguimec Bridge'   Jane Tims

bunches of bitter

    Ellis Bridge
    North Becaguimec River #4

beside the Ellis Bridge
choke-cherries hang in mist
and berries blacken

R.S., E L O
who were they?
Braxton, KAMRYN
S M, G M P

did they wade the shallow water?
fish for trout?
shout and listen for echo?

did they strip berries from branches?
pucker lips and cheeks?
does Eric still love Linda? [19]

---

[19] Ellis Bridge is on an out-of-the-way road in the hilly wooded area north of Carlisle in Carleton County. The bridge was built in 1909 and crosses the North Becaguimec Stream, a tributary of the St. John River. Becaguimec means 'the place where the salmon lie,' named *A-bek-a-gwim'-ek* by the Wolastoqiyik people for a salmon pool at the mouth of the river. The Ellis Bridge is the only one remaining of the covered bridges that once crossed the Becaguimec.

Jan. 5, 2012   'Hairy Woodpecker'   © Jane Tims

kissing bridge

covered bridge, a resonance
chamber, timbre intensified
a car engine, laughter
the rumble of tires

vibration of boards, loosened
birdsong, nest building
hammer-hollow of a woodpecker
patter of woodchips

breath, heartbeat, footfall
giggle, lips press and separate
a shout – *goodnight*
heading home for supper

echoes gentle
bolts creak
timbers settle

grit of a blade
letters in wood
shavings, brushed
from the groove

engraver hums
riff to a love song
a whisper, to rafters given
and amplified

Dec. 20, 2011   'Chickadee'   © Jane Tims

'PHOEBE'

    Wheaton Bridge
    Tantramar River #2

carved name
in the bridge
PHOEBE

Black-capped Chickadee pipes
fee -bee, hey-sweetie
(bored with *chick-a-dee-dee-dee*)

and Eastern Phoebe
black bed-head, dirty throat
rasps *fee-bee, whee-zy*

PHOEBE
nudges her way
into Monday [20]

---

[20] The Wheaton Bridge has stood since 1916 over the meandering Tantramar River on High Marsh Road in the lonely expanses of the Tantramar Marshes of Westmorland County. We found the name Phoebe carved on the timbers of the Wheaton Bridge when we visited it in April, 1992. When we revisited the bridge in 2015, the carving was gone.

'LANA + ...'

MacFarlane Bridge
Ward's Creek #2

who
LANA
loved is now
lost, a remnant
of story, carving
incomplete in chain
of robin song, the lament
of mourning dove, a kenning
creek blood over stone, flight-tilted
semaphore of swallows, purple poetry
phlox along the shore, whispers – the weeks
she waited, told no one, fingered the hem of her dress [21]

---

[21] MacFarlane Bridge crosses Ward's Creek, a tributary of the Kennebecasis River, near Sussex Corner. Ward's Creek is narrow and tea-coloured, tucked into lush vegetation. The bridge was built in 1909 and is richly carved with names and initials. The bridge is located on a busy country road with forested land to the east and agricultural land to the west. Mounds of weedy fall phlox grow at the edges of fields along the creek.

A kenning is a poetic expression from Anglo-Saxon and Viking origins – in its simplest form, a compound phrase expressing a metaphor replaces a single noun.

forever

we stand, tip-toe
on the roof of the truck
deep-carve initials
into the timbers of the bridge
stifle giggles, pledge to endure
blink, brush curls of wood
from our foreheads

hurry

brakes squeal
and silence
exposed wood
gleams in the tail-lights
left to mist and dark
years will grey the letters
weather the words

Jan. 26, 2016   'thistles - Malone Bridge'   Jane Tims

confluence

    Malone Bridge
    Kennebecasis River #23

headwaters of the Kennebecasis –
merge and gurgle, shade and shadow
of two brooks, and winds
spill along the valley, meet
as a breeze inside the bridge

framed by woodland, roadside tansy
bull thistle and a field of goldenrod
a few houses, a homestead
fences and an orchard
remnants of community

at either end of the bridge
an apple tree, an elm
the apple leans over the water
green fruit smooth
as river stone

this was their meeting place –
she lived in Goshen
he walked the long road from South Branch
his name on the beam
hers in the rafters [22]

---

22   Malone Bridge, on the isolated Goshen Road near Upper Goshen in Kings County, was built in 1911. The remnants of the Malone homestead, established 1820, are located near the bridge. At this point the Kennebecasis is a narrow, clear stream. The two brooks that seem to come together at the bridge are actually two braids of the same river.

'LEIK 1931'

Smyth Bridge
South Oromocto River #2

river water sparkles
in August sun, light leaks
between gable boards
through squares cut high in the walls

    chill within
    carved initials
    and the focused presence
    of ghosts with knives
    grey boards
    webbed by spider

then, the clatter
of tires on timbers
as a car rattles
across the bridge [23]

---

[23] The square openings, cut at intervals near the top of the bridge wall, are used to support scaffolding during bridge repairs.

black horse

> Pont Lavoie
> Quisibis River #2

at midnight
Sophie walks
to the covered bridge, carries
a flashlight and a makeup brush
a pot of black paint

captures him
in long strokes
and simple lines
steps back

> *tempting to give in*
> *to opportunity*
> *dab initials or random*
> *graffiti on blank canvas*
> *clean the brush*
> *on boards*

but she has done
what she came to do

black horse
crossed here once
clatter of hooves
on the wooden floor [24]

---

24 Pont Lavoie was built in 1951 on the Deschénes Road near Sainte-Anne-de-Madawaska, Madawaska County. On the day we visited, the roadside near the bridge was a riot of wildflowers – purple clover, ox-eye-daisy, bird's-foot trefoil and lupin.

crossing 1942

Nackawic Siding Bridge
Nackawic River #5

'I crossed this bridge over 70 years ago. with
horse and wagon Mavis August 25th, 2012'

— note in black ink on the walls of the
Nackawic Siding Bridge

clatter of hooves, a drum-roll
cart wheels rumble and Charlie reaches
with finger tips, to touch the rafter
Sit down, says Daniel

Faster, says Charlie, *Faster!*
Walk your horse, says Daniel
Save the fine! the horses in no hurry
to leave this facsimile of barn

safe from the rush and riffle of river
a pause in the pitch and roll of the wagon
through the window a glimpse
of steep bank and cedar

Charlie shouts to hear echoes
Daniel tightens the reins
big wheels step from the bridge
long hill ahead, bridge behind [25]

---

25 The Nackawic Siding Bridge, built in 1927, crosses the Nackawic River near Millville, York County. Today the bridge is very isolated and the road to reach it is rough and rocky.

holes

    Moores Mills Bridge
    Trout Creek #5

they drive in, write
'Just Married'
in white chalk
drive out

on the cross-brace
pileated woodpecker hammers
inspects the siding
excavates for bugs

ASH COLE admires
its red crest, carves
his name in caps
plays hockey at the rink
on the north side of the bridge
hits the ski hill on weekends

new cedar shingles cover
gaps in roofing
repel the rain
boards dry, even live knots
loosen, pop, splash
float downriver

high in the wall
a bullet hole
above the heads
of skating children [26]

---

[26] The Moores Mills Bridge over Trout Creek, a tributary of the Kennebecasis River, was built in 1923 near Sussex, Kings County. The bridge is in a sheltered valley, on an isolated road surrounded by woods. The road leads to an outdoor skating rink. A pileated woodpecker beat on the high edge of the entryway while we were there. This large woodpecker has a bright red crest on his head. The bullet hole and the neatly carved name ASH COLE were memorable markings in the bridge.

throb

> Milkish Inlet #1

staples sting
stipple the gable end
notices of strawberry suppers
weddings and rallies

paper tatters and horse manure
first of many signs of human occupation
traffic relentless
cars take turns

a fisherman, in an orange shirt
snags waterweed from the inlet
and visitors yodel
how old are these boards?

swimmers kick out
the walls on one side
water the perfect depth
for a cannonball or dive

knife wounds too
WALTER BROWN
Dunk and Lacke
1937

salt wind whistles
in old woodpecker cavities
roams through rafters
a bumblebee busy in the vetch [27]

---

[27] At Bayswater on the Kingston Peninsula, Kings County, the Milkish Inlet Bridge crosses an arm of the Milkish Channel of the St. John River. The two-span bridge was built in 1920 to replace a drawbridge, so some of those boards have been there for almost 100 years. The name Milkish comes from the Wolastoqiyik name *A-mil'-kesk*, meaning 'the place where fish or meat is preserved or cured.' The sounds of flowing water and wind echo in the eaves of the bridge.

a blade of grass between thumbs

> "...Hark the gossip of the grasses
> Bivouacked beneath the moon!"
>
> Charles G. D. Roberts
> "Afoot"

conjunction – February 21, 2015

    Patrick Owens Bridge
    Rusagonis River #2

Venus and Mars
sickle of mid-winter moon
planet and moon light scamper
into crevasses

headlights of the half-ton enter
overwhelm planet shadow
startle a winter hare
erect on haunches, paw lifted

frosted by sky-gaze, worshiping
the sliver of moon, dismayed
at desecration, round glare
of the truck's predatory eyes

fright to stop a heart
or flight to mobilize
hind-legs straighten
before fore-legs turn

long ear shadows
quit the length of the bridge
ahead of whiskers, chin velvet
and rabbit wisdom [28]

---

[28] On the evening of Feb. 21, 2015, Venus and Mars were in conjunction, very near to the waxing crescent moon. A conjunction is the alignment of planets or other celestial objects, making them appear to be at the same place in the sky. On this night it was impossible to ignore the mythology of the moon-gazing hare.

ptarmigan hunter

    Nackawic Siding Bridge
    Nackawic River #5

        'Ptarmigan Hunter
        Ray Brown
        May 12, 1896
        Horse had bad leg'

    – printed in black in the bridge

an expert birder tells me
ptarmigan have never been seen
in New Brunswick

so I must assume
Ray Brown hunted his ptarmigan
in more tundra-like places

but perhaps that May
as he crossed the bridge
with his limping horse

he scanned these blue woods
for the ghost of a plump bird
mottled with white

feathered feet and toes
the downward pull of saplings
buds of birch and willow catkins

listened for a chuckle
or a cluck
over the gurgle of the rapidy brook

took aim [29]

---

[29] Although the Nackawic Siding Bridge was built in 1927, we found this notation, with the date 1896, in the bridge when we visited in 1992. In 2012 the note about the ptarmigan was gone. Carvings and other markings are sometimes lost to souvenir hunters but more often when boards are replaced for bridge maintenance.

'TOM MOUSE' #1

    Bell Bridge
    South Oromocto River #3

runs along wooden
joists, keeps close-tucked
to the outer wall

nibbles a crumb from a bag
of cheezies tossed
from an open window

sips beer from a blue
aluminum can, scrapes
wax from a paper

coffee cup, carves
his two names
on the slanted beam

teeth chisel the letters
takes years to finish
the 'M's

who knew a mouse
could leave a comment?

'TOM MOUSE' #2

    Bell Bridge
    South Oromocto River #3

checked the phone book –
no Mouse between Murphy
and Moss.

perhaps this mouse:

    studied the initials
    of the high school team
    carved when the bus
    stopped on the way home
    from a game.

    found letters in the
    wind-nudges of contrails
    against blue sky.

    listened carefully
    to well-informed
    barn swallows.

puzzled out white
grease-paint notations
on the brown lids
of empty coffee cups.

peered at alphabet
books on the laps of children
in the back seats of cars
out for Sunday drives.

kindergarten graduate
or home-schooled – you have to admire
the matriculation of a white-footed mouse
educated in a covered bridge.

wind enters

    Smyth Bridge
    South Oromocto River #2

shaped by river, held as a blade of grass
between thumbs, wall boards whistle, twist and turn
air travels reed, over and under, braces, struts and beams

wedged into eaves, a dry leaf chatters
irritant above the slap and gurgle of water
over quartz, gravels mumble, rocks connect

deliberate woodpecker staccato
drills keyholes in soffit of gable ends
squeal of tires leaves black prints on the deck

we honk as we pass halfway
we exit
wind enters

April 14, 2016 'lichen garden' Jane Tims

time-stamped

>Pont Lavoie
>Quisibis River #2

when the end-post
of the guard rail
(pressure-treated)
splits and rots
the broken space
makes room
for rain and pollen
dust and autumn leaves
other detritus

spores find encouragement
and long-lived lichens grow
Cladonia cristatella
(soldier lichen), uniformed in red
blue-grey *Cladina* (reindeer lichen)
and pyxie cups

bridge not meant
to last forever

June 18, 2016   'web'   Jane Tims

a spider waits

    Ellis Bridge
    North Becaguimec River #4

she weaves and sets her snare
between the posts, and confident, the spider waits

cedar shingles, boards replaced and rafters new
but traffic sparse, and in the web the spider waits

aster, shepherd's purse and mullein crowd the road
no risk from the press of tires, and the spider waits

years since they wrote their names inside the bridge
crickets sing, and in its web the spider waits

after the flood, drifts of birch and maple high
on the river shore, the spider mends its web and waits

skater bug steps on the river's skin, fears
the dry of the river bed, and in its web the spider waits

on aging crib work velvet moss and lichens grow
landscape formed on rotting wood, and the spider waits

samara storm

> Darlings Island Bridge

walk the parquet floor
of the covered bridge
drifted with maple keys

imagine
samara storm
slant of helicopter blade

seeds enter the bridge
cycle down
settle where

earth and sun and water
dwindle to rarity
reproductive success unlikely

smooth seed and wing
lie useless, wish for a wind
or a broom to sweep clean [30]

---

[30] A samara, also known as a key, is a winged fruit. The samara of the red maple allows the seed to auto-rotate and travel long distances from the parent tree.

'I AM THE WIND'

    Stillwater Bridge
    Digdeguash River #2

I am the wind
   of the Digdeguash
   shaped by valley walls

I race trout
   lift ferns
   blow quick kisses
   under the wings of butterflies

I am the wind
   spoken in the beams
   of the covered bridge
   slipped into space
   between
   boards

I rattle the roof, the reeds
   vibrate with my breath

I am the wind
  from the County line
  to the Passamaquoddy Bay
  refreshed by waterfalls, salted
  by rising tide

I carve my name
on the boards, block
my name in yellow
chalk

I AM THE WIND [31]

---

[31] The Stillwater Bridge, built in 1901 over the Digdeguash River near Digdeguash in Charlotte County, no longer exists. After burning on Hallowe'en night in the early 1990s it was replaced by a metal Bailey Bridge. In 1992 we found the words 'I AM THE WIND' written in chalk on many of the covered bridges in Charlotte County. The Digdeguash River flows into Passamaquoddy Bay.

mystery

    McCann Bridge
    Digdeguash River #4

we puzzle under ropes and chains
a steel cable with a hook
hung from the cross-beams

perhaps:

a rope swing inside the bridge after midnight

a suicide pact

a hanging

ghouls strung from rafters at Hallowe'en

a challenge – the timed climb of a knotted rope

a hammock slung, cool snooze to the trill of cicadas

a banner draped at graduation

other evidence:

three dozen names and initials
scribbled, printed and cursive
on boards and beams
with pen and pencil
knife and nail

gaps between boards

"… The warping boards pull out their own old nails …"

Robert Frost
"The Black Cottage"

ceiling of stars

> Smyth Bridge
> South Oromocto River #2

Left to the years
to frost heaves, wind
and winter storms,
the roof-skin peels
away.

Gaps between boards,
layers criss-crossed,
flawless squares.
Sunlight squeezes
through

sketches
noonday constellations.
On dark days rain
drops ooze, saucepans
could catch drips.

Deafening –
would startle swallows,
field mice, snowshoe
hares, spiders,
and other star gazers. [32]

---

[32] At the time of our visit, the shingles were missing from the roof and the spaces between the boards left the impression of a starry sky.

push

> Oldfield Bridge
> Smith Creek #5

projected from a knothole
in the wall, a light trembles
on the wooden floor, a flashlight
searches, who grows there?

by a window, blocked over
slits between grey boards
light and dark, wet and dry
not quite touching

squeeze between boards
push through to blue-lined valley
serviceberry leans, petals fall
splay across layered slate

brookwater on stone
a dandelion, one toe in the road
ant hills in wheel tracks
and horsetails risk the press

of a treaded tire
grasses bend beneath
the thick persistent reed
of the valley wind [33]

---

[33] The Oldfield Bridge, near Newtown, Kings County, crosses Smith Creek, a tributary of the Kennebecasis River. The bridge was built in 1910. Cedar and hemlock are common trees along the steep and wooded shore. The trickle of water and the rush of wind dominate the experience of standing in the bridge. The bridge is on a side road, not busy, and horsetails, coltsfoot and anthills encroach into the road.

A monument near the entrance of the bridge was erected in 1992, during the 125th anniversary of Canada, to recognise the bridge 'as an integral part of New Brunswick's heritage.' The image of a 25 cent coin showing the Oldfield Bridge is carved into the monument, New Brunswick's contribution to a special commemorative coin set issued in 1992.

carving

    Urney Bridge
    Trout Creek #4

four lines incised
on the beam –
a bridge within a bridge

bridge over the river
sound of rocks under water
gravels adjusting to one another

he carved these lines
folded his knife
sat, spine against timber

listened to the water
thrashing rock, gravels
adjusting to one another

this year the freshet
undermined the abutment
coltsfoot leaves took hold

on the embankment
pulse of the river, gravels
adjusting to one another

March 6, 2016 'among the beams' Jane Tims

surveillance

    Burpee Bridge
    Gaspereau River #2

barn swallows in the rafters worry
fret and agitate
    humans in the bridge
    lean on the window ledge
    shout names, suggest vagaries
foam floats
slips beneath the bridge
river tea-coloured and cinnamon

swallows launch
dart, perturbed
    wing-tips skim cross-beams
    bank and navigate
    cliffs along the river
slate-blue backs
forked tails
peet and *p-tweet*

swallows hunker down

watch, vigilant, know

    humans with blue spray paint

    climb as high as nests

    daubed on timbers

one broken on the roadway

swirl of grasses

feathers, mud [34]

---

[34] Built in 1913, the Burpee Bridge crosses the Gaspereau River, near Gaspereau Forks, Queens County. The name of the river is from the French for the Gaspereau fish found there. The water, draining the tannin-rich boglands to the north and west, is reddish in colour. The river is bordered by mixed wood and the approach to the bridge is bordered by a grove of grey birch. On one side the river banks are steep, layered cliffs. The river is a wide floodplain at this point divided by 'islands' of shallow gravel and silt. The inside of the bridge is striped with bird guano and marked with bright graffiti.

break-in #1

> Burpee Bridge
> Gaspereau River #2

1.
barn swallow nest
powdered wreck of grass and clay
knocked from the rafters

swallow tried to frighten the vandal
wing dip, sideways presentation
of beak and feathers

dives and near-misses
like markings on moth wings
unblinking predatory eyes

swallow quits the bridge
finds a gap between barn boards
new grasses, new clay

2.
muddy boot print on the outer door
papers scrambled, broken dishes
nothing taken

I change the locks, install cameras
motion detectors, put 911 on speed-dial
paint angry eyes on the backs of lawn chairs

I erect signposts:
vicious dog, beware
house for sale

break-in #2

> Burpee Bridge
> Gaspereau River #2

barn swallow nest, sad rubble, grass and clay
knocked to the carriageway
third nest this year

muddy boot print on the outer door, smashed handle
papers scattered, broken drawers
barn swallow nest, sad rubble, grass and clay

swallow turns silhouette sideways to the vandal
angry twitter, skewed flight and feather flare
third nest this year

a deception, the way markings on moth wings reveal
predatory eyes, mimic and dare
barn swallow nest, sad rubble, grass and clay

I change locks, place cameras in rafters, put 911 on speed-dial
paint angry faces on lawn chairs
third nest this year

the bird quits the bridge, the broken nest-tangle
gathers new mud, new grass, new ditch flowers
barn swallow nest, sad rubble, grass and clay
third nest this year

'chikin'

>McGuire Bridge
>Digdeguash River #3

1.
a single word
in felt-tipped pen
'chikin'
edits needed –
change the second 'i' to 'e '
and add a 'c'

2.
boards kicked
a fifth of the southern, downstream wall
now a window

fear of heights, brave
to stand at the opening, only a two by four
between me and river

islands of thin foam pass
beneath sharp thorns on hawthorn, choke cherries
dogwood doll's eyes

white asters, bracken, goldenrod
guttation drops on leaves of strawberry, dust on yarrow
clovers – rabbit's foot, red and sweet

wish I was downstream
on the sandbar, safe by the fire, seated
on the driftwood log [35]

---

35 The McGuire Bridge, built in 1913, crosses the Digdeguash River in Elmsville, near St. George, Charlotte County. Deposits of sandy gravel line the river shore and the water is amber with tannins. During our September visit fall flowers filled the ditches leading to the bridge – goldenrods, pearly everlasting and Queen Anne's lace.

'AJS 1932'

    Marven Bridge
    Belleisle Creek #2

what makes the bridge shake?

sound waves from blue jay and bull frog
the weight and glare of graffiti
paper nests where bald-faced hornets
squeeze in and leave

lichened boards, loosened
mortise and tenon disarticulated
nails rattled free from purlins and sills
beams with weakened braces

the shock of seeing my initials
and an impossible date

last week's discarded bones of a bear
dumped over the abutment, tibia and fibula
disassociated, tendons and ligaments
peeled from joints and processes

ribs and sternum, glisten
pelvis and scapula, gristled
without the sculpted elegance
of weathered bone [36]

---

[36] Marven Bridge, over Belleisle Creek since 1903, is located on the little-used Swamp Road near Springfield, Kings County. When we walked inside, the bridge shook. Inside the bridge is decorated with graffiti and some older carvings, including the initials in the title of the poem. We saw lots of wild life signs at this bridge. The black flies were vicious and hornets had built nests inside the bridge. The carcass was a disconcerting reminder of the isolation.

wobble

    Marven Bridge
    Belleisle Creek #2

bridge shudders as we walk
lights on floor, staccato, gaps between boards
photos out of focus, faint tremble

cribwork and rafters, new wood
but old nails work loose, purlins frail
bridge shakes as we walk

in the rafters, the paper nest of a wasp
in the mud, ephemeral, the tracks of fox
photos out of focus, faint tremble

a blue jay calls *thief,* skims brown water
at the shoreline, sensitive fern
bridge shivers as we walk

on the ledge, bones, picked-clean
skeleton of a bear, backbone and fingers
photos out of focus, faint tremble

orange graffiti, letters round and wide
initials on the beams eroded
bridge quivers as we walk
photos out of focus, faint tremble

dry wood

    Adair Bridge
    North Becaguimec River #1

Adair Bridge, roofed
kept timbers and jackets
dry, the way a paper box
protects wooden matches.

an hour after midnight, the fire
fighters watch, nothing they can do.
rocks steam
roof sags
roadway
almost
touches
river.

dry wood
resists rot,
dry wood
makes tinder,

match between fingers.
strike the sulphurous end
on the cardboard box
kept dry in a jacket
pocket.

often walked home
after midnight.
often in rain.
had to cross
the river.
bridge
covered. [37]

---

[37] The Adair Bridge, in Cloverdale, Carleton County, was built in 1948 to cross the North Becaguimec Steam. It was destroyed by fire in October 2009.

Aaron Clark Bridge on the Canaan River

Canaan River   No. 1

A groan, a splinter and she rips from her foundation, lists to one side, sets off on her ride. She's bound for an April lark on the Canaan, tea-coloured, flood-quick, in a hurry. Alders and birches swept aside, two hour freedom, twenty kilometer rafting ride. People watch from the shore, shake heads. *Courted in that bridge. Walk over every day to see my sister. Kids run the 164 foot span like laps in a pool. Saves a twenty minute drive the long way round.*

But the river's push
is not sentimental.

Downriver, the bridge fetches up on a concrete pier,
                                    the Trans-Canada
                                                Highway.

At recovery
she is dismembered, piece by piece
Forty feet of her stored to spend
months in the dark,
not knowing the future [38]

---

[38] On April 16, 2014, floodwaters ripped the Aaron Clark Bridge from its abutments. The bridge was built to cross the Canaan River in 1927 on Cherryvale Road, east of Canaan Forks, Queens County.

cars discouraged

    Nackawic Siding Bridge
    Nackawic River #5

Siding Road to Woodman
eroded, rocky, overgrown
alders and grey birch lean
mast year for maple keys
every last one sprouted
the bridge more potting shed
than crossing

and above, a flock of starlings
a murmuration lured
by the plethora of seed

a loose board rattles

> "… The gurgling growl of the muddy tide
> Creeps up by the bridge's leaning side …"
>
> Mary Electa Adams
> "By the Marshes of Tantramar"

May 12, 2012 'enter' Jane Tims

dry wind

> French Village Bridge
> Hammond River #2

the bridge leans, upriver
wind enters, a beer can
rolls on the deck

white butterflies obey
the valley breeze
navigate the scent of wild roses

avoid the dogs
cooling off in the river
the beach folk, sunning themselves

bracts of Yellow Rattle
and *Silene*, inflated bladders
dry as old boards

aspens tremble
a song sparrow stutters
a loose shingle rattles in wind

sound of the mill

Tomlinson Mill Bridge
Odellach River #2

osier dogwood, red leaves turn
the planer at the saw mill winding

drawn-out caw of a harried crow
the planer at the saw mill binding

pair of woodpeckers, red heads, perch
the planer at the saw mill grinding

fall rain rattles on the corrugated roof
the planer at the saw mill whining

phantom splash of the mill race
the planer at the saw mill pining [39]

---

[39] The bridge at Tomlinson Mill near Arthurette is the only covered bridge remaining in Victoria County. It was built in 1918 and crosses the Odellach River. The river is pale amber and rocky-bottomed, and the shore is lined with birch and other hardwood. The mill is in a large open area at one end of the bridge and the concrete walls of the old mill race are visible along the bank of the river.

posters

    Plumweseep Bridge
    Kennebecasis River #9

mounds of yellow bedstraw, cucumber vine
upstream a silver riffle, downstream a sign
for conservation, tacked in a dead elm tree
reminds anglers – 'set young salmon free'

hawthorn, piercing spines and ripening berries
goldenrod and drupes of purple cherry
a truck drives into the bridge, a thud
an angler's tracks, pressed into sandy mud

grey boards, ragged edge above the brook
the angler tugs the rod, sets the hook
rabbit's foot clover, Queen Anne's tatted lace
he snags a hank of pickerel weed, his face

weary, packs his tackle, trudges home
heads of timothy, a metronome [40]

---

40 The Plumweseep Bridge is located near Sussex, Kings County. It was built in 1911 and crosses the Kennebecasis River. The name Plumweseep is a combination of the Wolastoqiyik words *plumwe* for 'salmon' and *seep* for 'river.' Many efforts are underway to restore the waning salmon population in the Kennebecasis River system.

'line of pigeons on the Florenceville Bridge' Jane Tims

keeping watch

Florenceville Bridge

pigeons swim through air
fill gaps on the ridge line

perch on the shingled roof
scrutinize the traffic
the squeeze of half-tons
on the bridge
the kissing of mirrors

pigeons quit the ridge, glide
to the shore of the *Wolastoq*

river winds shiver
hawkweed and sumac, displace
blankets of wild cucumber, billow
the skirts and Tilley
hats of tourists [41]

---

41 The Florenceville Bridge in Florenceville, Carleton County is one of two covered bridges that now cross the St. John River. When it was built in 1907, there were five covered spans; today only one of these remains and four are made of steel trusses. The Wolastoqiyik people named the river *Wolastoq* meaning 'the good or handsome river (for canoe navigation).'

pastoral

>Centreville Bridge
>Millstream River #5

white farm houses
green pasture

truck from the River Association
bundles of bank willow cuttings

logs in the stream to dig
new habitat for fishes

fifteen years since they planted
rows of conifers

to keep the herd
and mud from the stream

cows white and black
one watching, curious [42]

---

[42] The Centreville Bridge, near Berwick, Kings County, was built in 1911 and crosses the Millstream River, a tributary of the Kennebecasis. The efforts of the Kennebecasis Watershed Restoration Committee (KWRC) were evident at the bridge: trees planted in the riparian area, digger logs installed in the stream to provide habitat diversity, and a KWRC truck, filled with bundles of bank willow cuttings ready to plant.

family drive, when we were five

Hartland Bridge

enter the narrow, eyes adjust
shout and echo, taunt of an imp
in the rafters, air drawn in and held
bad luck to breathe inside the bridge

longest breath, dad's
his foot above the gas, hovers
his broad grin in the rear-view mirror
from entrance to exit

squint, park the car, run back
feet slap on boards
beyond the wall tires rumble
a single honk, elbows on sill

pebbles to amber water, the splash
carried down-stream, whir
of pigeon wings, the feathered
roof of the bridge [43]

---

43 At 391 metres, the Hartland Bridge is the longest covered bridge in the world. It was built at Hartland, Carleton County, in 1901 to cross the St. John River but was not covered until 1921. The bridge includes a side passage for pedestrians. Trying to hold your breath as you cross the bridge is a local custom.

April 18, 2016 'pickerel weed - Canal Bridge' Jane Tims

disarranged

Canal Bridge

the river –
    bogun-brown, crossed
    by a bridge, roofed with lily pads
    and water shield, edged
    with pondweed, purple heads
    of pickerel weed
    point downstream

the walls –
    boards missing, spaces
    patched, vertical and horizontal
    unified by nails and the mourning call
    of a dove in the rafters
    on the deck, a crack of egg shell
    an ecru feather

a spider web –
    covered bridge caught
    in strands, snagged in rafters
    slung across the truss
    stirred by the breath
    of a blue van crossing [44]

---

[44] The Canal Bridge in Charlotte County crosses a branch of the Magaguadavic River draining Lake Utopia. Occasionally, when water levels are high, the river flows in reverse, into the lake. The name Magaguadavic comes from the Wolastoqiyik and Passamaquoddy name *Mag-ee-eeat-a'-wik* meaning 'river of big eels.'

delay

>Urney Bridge
>Trout Creek #4

covered bridge –
      a leaf inverted
       to repel the rain
roof keeps rafters
and underpinnings dry

but damp prevails

rotation of shingles and sheet metal
every year the wall boards grey
gouges from logging trucks
mow the ditches and next year branches
brush the gables

discouraging really

sunscreen and canvas hats

respiration

    Wheaton Bridge
    Tantramar River #2

"... Over the lines of the dykes, over the gossiping grass ..."
                Charles G. D. Roberts, "Tantramar Revisited"

the bridge is a lung
    breathes
      out and in
for birds and lichens
and marshes and me

the bridge inhales
    the shrill wind
      is a train whistle
one last look
from the window

a muskrat tows
a 'V' on the water
    dives and surfaces for air

I am birdsong and frog-swallow
a wingbeat
saltfresh and shallow

I sit on the abutment
  and sigh
and orange *Xanthoria*
gleans nutrients
from the seabreeze

the bridge exhales
  grasses and feathers and I
  smoothed over
where Acadian dykes
still dry the land [45]

---

[45] The Tantramar Marshes were originally salt marsh, converted to agricultural use by a system of sluices and dykes built by the Acadians. The name *Tantramar* means 'a thundering noise or racket,' from the Acadian French *tintamarre*, after the noise of the river or the flocks of noisy birds feeding in the marshlands. The whistle of the wind in the bridge dominates all other sounds. While we were at the bridge, a horse drawn wagon brought tourists across the bridge.

Xanthoria is a bright gold or orange foliose lichen living on rock or wood in coastal and agricultural areas.

dark mirror

> Starkey Bridge
> Long Creek #1

river, dark mirror of leaves and stems
telephone line is cursive on water
simmer of wind and water strider

waves slip beneath the bridge, mellow
moons, verdigris on silver
river, dark mirror of leaves and stems

peepers, faint frog splash and echo
black and white scat, deft climber
summer of wind and water strider

a chalky mound of droppings, swallow
nest above, in rafters
river mud, matter of leaves and stems

water shield and wild rice
anthers are pink chandeliers
shimmer of wind and water strider

cricket song and conversations with crows
red wings in the alders, dabblers
in river, dark mirror of leaves and stems
quiver of wind and water strider [46]

---

46 Starkey Bridge, built in 1912, crosses a marshy area of Long Creek near Coles Island in Queens County. The Wolastoqiyik name for the creek is *Nem-mutch-i-pscut'-quac* meaning 'dead water.'

maintenance

    Urney Bridge
    Trout Creek #4

the covered bridge
a stepping stone

if only those who cross here
would move more slowly
take care not to gouge
the walls, the sides
not leave wounds in wood

a mackerel sky
means rain in twenty-four hours
every stepping stone
an inch beneath the water

shifts a little
with the shear
unsettles in its cradle
steps less certain

some pull over
after they cross the bridge
wander inward
touch the wounded wood
wish life could last
a little longer

renewal

Moosehorn Creek #1.5

the bridge, retired
what to do?
without cars
the rumble of boards
the wear of tires

grass, brambles, saplings
peer inside
see possibility
in soil wedged
between decking

voices echo
and a path wears
between grasses
one sneaker
following another [47]

---

47 No longer in service, Moosehorn Creek #1.5 crosses the creek on an unused road, now grown-over. The bridge, built in 1915, is used as a park, accessible from a parking area and a tunnel under Route 1, near Bloomfield, Kings County. The name is descriptive, derived from the Wolastoqiyik *Moose-sum-wee-see-book* meaning 'moose's horn brook.'

morning

    Tranton Bridge
    Smith Creek #1

swallow twitter
tucks into angles
of end post and beam
folds back a corner on silence

bank beaver parts
a zipper on the satin of river
sets free a feather storm
of birdsong

blackpoll warbler
a chirp and a trill
curious in the maze
of alder branches

a red-wing, *chortle-dee*
an Eastern Towhee, *too-whee*
a goldfinch, delirious
a black-throated green

a stony path flows
beneath the bridge
cattle, released to pasture
line up to drink [48]

---

[48] Tranton Bridge. near Roachville, Kings County, was constructed in 1927. It crosses Smith Creek, tributary to the Kennebecasis River. The flat floodplain is part of the surrounding farmland. Fencing, cattle trails and bank willows line the water edge. The day of our visit, the valley was restless with bird calls, songs intensified by the enclosed space created by the wooden bridge.

thalweg

    Patrick Owens Bridge
    Rusagonis River #2

after two days of snow a deer
sews a seam on the river, solitary
trail on snow-covered ice

hooves planted deep and lifted
no hurry, follows the river
from the beaver dam

passes under the bridge
then to the forks where she takes
the North Branch

a search for open water
her track follows the thalweg
deepest channel

no acknowledgement
of bridge, not a veer
or stagger

no pause to look up
her trail reconnects
the interruption of landscape

Afterword

There are times in publishing when a book project clicks into place like the words of a poem that have been honed to a perfect fit. This has been our experience at Chapel Street Editions in working with Jane Tim's new book, *in the shelter of the covered bridge*.

After we published her first book of poems and drawings, *within easy reach*, which is about finding and gathering wild and domestic foods, she told us about her covered bridge project. When her new manuscript of poems and natural history notes, and her new folio of drawings came in, it was clear Jane's focus made the book a perfect fit for Chapel Street Editions.

When we started Chapel Street Editions we set our compass on a course for telling stories from the natural history and cultural life of the St. John River Valley. *In the shelter of the covered bridge* falls like a plumb line into the middle of our mandate. We could well take it as a flagship book for our publishing company. It certainly is a flagship book for Jane Tims. Reading this book reminded me of the famous lines by Emily Dickinson:

> There is no Frigate like a Book
>
> To take us Lands away
>
> Nor any Coursers like a Page
>
> Of prancing Poetry.

The "lands away" to which Jane takes us in this new book, and in her previous book, are places in our home region that are the "far away close by." Thoreau, who mostly stuck close to home, wrote, "I have travelled a good deal in Concord." Jane Tims follows the same discipline – travelling widely close to home.

The unusual thing about *in the shelter of the covered bridge* is the unity of focus the poet-artist-biologist has achieved with this book. While each element of the book has its own narrative stance, the poems, the drawings, and the natural history notes come together in a way that has an appealing and satisfying unity for ear, eye, and mind.

Jane is not a poet who puts all her aesthetic eggs in one basket. She moves easily between modes of expression. She is a connoisseur of land and life, an emissary for the intertwining stories of natural history and human culture.

Readers attracted by the poems and drawings pick up a good deal of natural and cultural history as well. Readers attracted to the natural and cultural history have their knowledge graced with the sounds of wind and water, and with the images of plants and animals that live "in the shelter of the covered bridge."

With her poetic, artistic, and research skills steering the ship, Jane is now sailing out once again into the geographic by-ways and cultural history of the province. She has a similar book project under way on the environments and cultural settings of one-room schoolhouses. I have no doubt she will offer up another voyage for ear, eye, and mind, and that we will again be culturally enriched by her inspiration and good efforts.

Keith Helmuth
Chapel Street Editions

Notes on the Drawings

Figure 1. "green apples" (frontispiece) – At the south end of the Malone Bridge, branches of an old apple tree with golden-green apples leaned over the water. The oval holes between the wall boards are made by woodpeckers excavating for insects.

Figure 2. "tangle" (page 2) – The two varieties of rose at one end of the bridge each had a distinctive scent – at a distance these two scents mingled to create a third, another tangled element among many.

Figure 3. "Coltsfoot" (page 12) – Coltsfoot, yellow and dandelion-like at first glance, is one of the first flowers to bloom along the spring roadside. Later, in summer, its big leaves cover the soil in green.

Figure 4. "watching the bridge" (page 14) – On the misty day we visited, the bridge was still and solitary, personified by the deer watching us from the hayfields.

Figure 5. "Nymphaea" (page 22) – On the still pond, lily pads almost cover the surface. The white flowers of *Nymphaea* provide elegant contrast to *Nuphar*, the yellow pond-lilies.

Figure 6. "Yellow Pond-lily" (page 26) – The edges of Bloomfield Creek are marshy, inhabited by various species of aquatic flowering plants, the prettiest of these the yellow pond-lily, also called spatterdock.

Figure 7. "three studies of a groundhog" (page 28) – The groundhog in this drawing was busy going in and out of a culvert at The Pines Conservation Park in Cambridge Narrows. Not far away is the former site of the Narrows Covered Bridge – the Ground Hog Gale of 1976 reduced it to boards and splinters. A ferry crossed the Narrows for a short while before the new concrete bridge was constructed.

Figure 8. "tree swallow" (page 34) – A tree swallow was our companion in the Hoyt Station Bridge. The bird kept flying up and hitting the gable wall and she seemed confused and scared. Watching, we discovered this was her method of hunting the insects on the wall.

Figure 9. "hawk moth in lilac" (page 38) – The lilac and its busy population of hawk moths was the focal point for our visit to the Benton Bridge. From our visit in 1992, I remember a group of elevated nesting boxes and their busy population of purple martins, but these were gone in 2015.

Figure 10. "choke-cherries at Becaguimec Bridge" (page 44) – In mid-summer, the choke-cherries hang thick and dark along our roadsides in New Brunswick. Eaten from the bush, they are astringent and sour but they make excellent jelly.

Figure 11. "Hairy Woodpecker" (page 46) – This drawing is from my photo of a hairy woodpecker at our winter feeder. Lines of woodpecker excavations were a common sight at the covered bridges we visited.

Figure 12. "Chickadee" (page 48) – Most people know the chickadee's name-sake mnemonic, *chick-a-dee-dee-dee*. They may hear *fee-bee* and not realise the same bird is singing.

Figure 13. "thistles" (page 52) – The Malone Bridge, part of the landscape of the old homestead, seemed framed in flowers – bull thistle and Canada goldenrod, bladder campion and yellow hawkweed.

Figure 14. "conjunction" (page 64) – This is a fanciful image of the rabbit we saw at the Patrick Owens Bridge. My memory is of him running from the bridge, a startled flow of limbs, his long-eared shadow leading the way.

Figure 15. "Reeds and reflection" (page 72) – Reflections on water are very satisfying to draw. This drawing is of reeds growing just off the bridge at the Nerepis Marsh where the Nerepis River empties into the St. John River near Grand Bay-Westfield.

Figure 16. "lichen garden" (page 74) – The diversity and colours of the lichens in these 'gardens' create a charming vignette. You'd think they'd been planted!

Figure 17. "web" (page 76) – This drawing was inspired by a photo by Ed Post of Cox Ford Bridge, Indiana, of a rain-soaked spider's web.

Figure 18. "among the beams" (page 88) – Swallows were a common bird inside the covered bridges we visited. Their streaky white droppings were the most natural of any of the markings. Both barn swallows and cliff swallows use vegetation and mud to build nests in the rafters.

Figure 19. "enter" (page 106) – The river deposits sand upstream of the French Village Bridge, making it a popular place for swimming and wading. The sounds of song sparrows, crickets and cars honking as they cross the bridge compete with the purr of the wind and the rattle of loose boards.

Figure 20. "line of pigeons on the Florenceville Bridge" (page 110) – The line of pigeons on the ridge of the roof is a part of the silhouette of this bridge.

Figure 21. "pickerel weed – Canal Bridge" (page 114) – Pickerel weed, with its tall purple flower stalks, was thick along the shore of the Canal. In low water its leaves become flattened and disarranged as boats disturb the water.

Sources

Atkinson, Brian. *New Brunswick's Covered Bridges.* Halifax: Nimbus Publishing Limited: Halifax, 2010.

Boucher, Ray. *A Photo Tour of the Covered Bridges of New Brunswick.* Kissing Bridge Publications, 2009.

Coldrick, Helen. *New Brunswick's Covered Bridges.* Saint John: Neptune Publishing Company Limited, 1992.

Ganong, William F. "A Monograph of the Place-Nomenclature of the Province of New Brunswick", *Transactions of the Royal Society of Canada: Second Series 1896-97, Volumn II, Section II,* 1896.

Gillis, Stephen and John Gillis. *No Faster Than a Walk.* Fredericton: Goose Lane, 1988.

Harrington, Lyn and Richard Harrington. *Covered Bridges of Central and Eastern Canada.* Toronto: McGraw-Hill Ryerson Limited, 1976.

Provincial Archives of New Brunswick. *Place Names of New Brunswick: Where is Home? New Brunswick Communities Past and Present.* http://archives.gnb.ca/exhibits/communities/Home.aspx?culture=en-CA Accessed October 4, 2017.

The New Brunswick Department of Transportation and Infrastructure. Covered Bridges. http://www2.gnb.ca/content/gnb/en/departments/dti/bridges_ferries/content/covered_bridges.html Accessed October 4, 2017.

Sources for Epigraphs

Adams, Mary Electa. "By the Marshes of Tantramar", *From Distant Shores: Poems*. Toronto: 1898.

Browning, Elizabeth Barrett. "A Musical Instrument", *Poems Before Congress*. London: Chapman and Hall, 1860.

Doyle, Brian. *Covered Bridge*. Toronto: Groundwood Books Ltd., 1990.

Frost, Robert. "The Black Cottage", *North of Boston*. New York: Henry Holt and Co., 1917.

Frost, Robert. "West-Running Brook", *West-Running Brook*. New York: Henry Holt and Co., 1928.

Roberts, Charles G. D. "Afoot", *The Selected Poems of Sir Charles G. D. Roberts*. Toronto: McGraw-Hill Ryerson, 1974.

Roberts, Charles G. D. "Tantramar Revisited", *The Selected Poems of Sir Charles G. D. Roberts*. Toronto: Ryerson, 1936.

About the Author

Jane Spavold Tims is a botanist, historian, artist and writer. She was born and raised in southern Alberta and now lives in rural New Brunswick. She obtained her B.Sc. and M.Sc. in biology at Dalhousie University in Halifax and later returned to university to obtain a B.A. in anthropology and history at the University of New Brunswick in Fredericton. During her career she worked in environmental protection, in the fields of air quality, watershed management and community planning.

Jane writes poetry and fiction and presents her writing, painting and drawings of plants, birds and landscape at www.janetims.com. Her main interests include identifying plants, collecting wild foods and exploring New Brunswick's built heritage, including its covered bridges. She is a member of the Writers' Federation of New Brunswick (WFNB). Her manuscript "mnemonic", including some of the poems contained here, won the Alfred G. Bailey Prize in the 2016 WFNB Writing Competition.

Photo by J.D.R. Beaudoin

Her previous books include *within easy reach* (Chapel Street Editions, 2016), about wild edible and other local foods, and three books in the *Meniscus Series* of science fiction poetry (CreateSpace Independent Publishing Platform, 2017).

Jane believes in preserving our built heritage as an integral part of our landscape and ecology.

Index

Aaron Clark Bridge 101	McGuire Bridge 94
Adair Bridge 99	Milkish Inlet #1 60
Back Creek #2 . . . . 6, 35	Millstream River #5 112
Baker Brook #2 15	Moores Mills Bridge 58
Bell Bridge 8, 69, 70	Moosehorn Creek #1.5 121
Belleisle Creek #2 . . . . 96, 98	Nackawic River #5 . . . . .56, 67, 103
Benton Bridge 39, 40	Nackawic Siding Bridge 56, 67, 103
Bloomfield Creek Bridge 27	North Becaguimec River #1 99
Burpee Bridge 89, 91, 93	North Becaguimec River #4 . . . . . . 45, 77
Canaan River #1 101	Odellach River #2 108
Canal Bridge 115	Oldfield Bridge 85
Centreville Bridge 112	Patrick Owens Bridge 20, 23, 29, 65, 123
Darlings Island Bridge 3, 37, 78	Plumweseep Bridge 109
Digdeguash River #2 79	Pont Boniface 7
Digdeguash River #3 94	Pont Lavoie 55, 75
Digdeguash River #4 . . . . 36, 81	Quisibis River #2 . . . . 55, 75
Eel River #3 . . . . 39, 40	Rusagonis River #2 . . . .20, 23, 29, 65, 123
Ellis Bridge 45, 77	Salmon Bridge 32, 33
Florenceville Bridge 111	Smith Creek #1 122
French Village Bridge 5, 107	Smith Creek #5 85
Gaspereau River #2 . . . . 89, 91, 93	Smithtown Bridge 16
Green River #3 7	Smyth Bridge 42, 54, 73, 84
Hammond River #2 . . . . 5, 107	South Oromocto River #2 . . . . 42, 54, 73, 84
Hammond River #3 16	South Oromocto River #3 . . . . 8, 69, 70
Hartland Bridge 113	Starkey Bridge 119
Hoyt Station Bridge 6, 35	Stillwater Bridge 79
Kennebecasis #7.5 . . . . 32, 33	Tantramar River #2 . . . . .49, 117
Kennebecasis River #23 53	Tomlinson Mill Bridge 108
Kennebecasis River #9 109	Tranton Bridge 122
Long Creek #1 119	Trout Creek #4 . . . . 87, 116, 120
MacFarlane Bridge 50	Trout Creek #5 58
Malone Bridge 53	Urney Bridge 87, 116, 120
Marven Bridge 96, 98	Ward's Creek #2 50
McCann Bridge 36, 81	Wheaton Bridge 49, 117